THE BLUE ISLAND

Experiences of a New Arrival Beyond the Veil

Psychic photograph of
W. T. Stead given at Crewe, 1915.

THE BLUE ISLAND

Experiences of a New Arrival Beyond the Veil

Communicated by

W. T. STEAD

And recorded by

ESTELLE STEAD

With

PARDOE WOODMAN

WHITE CROW

www.whitecrowbooks.com

William Thomas Stead

Contents

~

The Psychic Life of
William Thomas Stead

∽

nown to the general public primarily as a dedicated journalist, author, social reformer, and pacifist, William Thomas Stead was on his way to New York to give a speech on world peace at Carnegie Hall when he became a victim of the *Titanic*.

Stead is remembered in psychic circles as the founder of *Borderland*, a quarterly journal devoted to psychical subjects, and as founder of Julia's Bureau, a psychic bureau intended to demonstrate the reality of survival after death as well as to assist in a spiritual revival. In 1891-92, stories from *Borderland* were compiled into two separate volumes – *Real Ghost Stories and More Ghost Stories*, and in 1897 they were published under one title, *Real*

Ghost Stories. These cases of apparitions, hauntings, astral projection, clairvoyance, and premonitions, collected by Stead, have since become a classic under the title *Borderland.* Stead was also an automatic writing medium when alive and a frequent spirit communicator after his death.

Born on July 5, 1849, at Embleton, Northumberland, England, Stead was first educated by his father, a Congregationalist minister, and later attended Silcoates School, Wakefield. In 1863, he became an office boy in a merchant's counting house in Newcastle-on-Tyne. The poems of James Russell Lowell played an important part in shaping his life's work, which, he decided, around age 18, was to help other people.

Stead's career as a journalist and author began during the 1860's when he became a reporter for a newspaper called the *Northern Echo,* advancing to editor in 1871. In 1880, he accepted a position as assistant editor of the *Pall Mall Gazette,* then became its editor in 1883. In 1890, he founded the *Review of Reviews.* According to Leslie Shepard, who wrote the Introduction to the New American Edition of *Borderland,* published in 1970, Stead is credited with inventing the "New Journalism," bringing important topics in bright, colourful prose to the man in the street. Shepard states that he introduced the interview technique to British journalism and was a pioneer of cheap reprints for mass sale in the form of penny pamphlets.

In a story written by B. O. Flower, the editor of *Arena,* a popular American publication, Stead is referred to as a cosmopolitan journalist "with a rare blending of intellectual force with moral conviction, idealism with utilitarianism, a virile imagination, and a common sense practicality that strove to make the vision a useful reality."

In one of his many stories, From the *Old World to the New*, a novel published in 1892, Stead described the sinking of a ship called the *Majestic* in the North Atlantic from hitting an iceberg. The name of the ship's captain was Edward J. Smith, the same name of the captain of the *Titanic*. In an 1886 story for The *Pall Mall Gazette*, Stead wrote about the sinking of an ocean liner and how lives were lost because there were too few lifeboats. Whether these two separate stories were precognition on Stead's part or merely coincidence is not known, but Stead apparently did not foresee the tragedy when he booked passage on the *Titanic*.

In 1909, three years before his death, he published *Letters from Julia*, a series of messages purportedly coming to Stead from Julia T. Ames, an American newspaperwoman, for her friend Ellen, during 1892-93. Stead had met both women on his travels, and several months after Julia's death, Ellen told Stead about seeing apparitions of Julia in her bedroom. Having recently discovered that he had the gift of automatic writing, Stead told Ellen that he would see if she could communicate through him. "Sitting alone with a tranquil mind, I consciously placed my right hand, with the pen held in the ordinary way, at the disposal of Julia, and watched with keen and skeptical interest to see what it would write," Stead explained in the book's Introduction. Julia's Bureau was formed that same year.

One survivor of the *Titanic* reported seeing Stead calmly sitting in the smoking room reading his Bible as other passengers scurried to the decks and the lifeboats. Another survivor recalled seeing Stead calmly holding back men who were attempting to board the lifeboats with the women and children. Stead was also remembered for having frequently discussed spiritual matters during meals on the *Titanic*.

Hester Travers Smith, a Dublin medium, recalled a sitting, on April 15, 1912, when she and a "Miss D." received a very rapid message stating: "Ship sinking; all hands lost. William East overboard. Women and children weeping and wailing – sorrow, sorrow, sorrow." They had no idea what the message meant and no more came through at that sitting. Later that day they heard that the *Titanic* had sunk. As a spirit claiming to be Stead communicated at subsequent sittings, Travers Smith concluded that because of the rapidity of the message they got the last name wrong the first time.

According to Rev. Charles L. Tweedale, the Church of England vicar of Weston, Stead appeared at a sitting given by Etta Wriedt in New York on April 17. Sir Arthur Conan Doyle, the physician who created Sherlock Holmes, called Wriedt the best direct-voice medium in the world and the plan was for Stead to accompany Wriedt back to England on his return voyage so that she could demonstrate her gift there. Wriedt made the trip without Stead and gave a sitting on May 6 in Wimbledon. In attendance were Vice-Admiral W. Usborne Moore and Estelle Stead, Stead's daughter. Moore reported that Stead talked with his daughter for at least 40 minutes. He described it as the most painful but most realistic and convincing conversation he had heard during his investigations of mediumship.

General Sir Alfred E. Turner reported that he held a small and private sitting at his home with Mrs. Wriedt. "We had hardly commenced when a voice, which apparently came from behind my right shoulder, exclaimed: 'I am so happy to be with you again,' Turner reported. "The voice was unmistakably that of Stead, who immediately began to tell us the events of the dire moments when the leviathan settled down. There was a short, sharp struggle to gain his breath and immediately afterwards he came to his senses in another stage of existence." At a later sitting with Wriedt, Turner saw Stead materialise, wearing his usual attire.

Tweedale also recorded that Stead was seen and heard on July 17, 1912 at the home of Professor James Coates of Rothesay, a well-known author and investigator, who had Mrs. Wriedt give a sitting with a number of witnesses. "Mr. Stead showed himself twice within a short time, the last appearance being clearly defined, and none will readily forget the clear, ringing tones of his voice," Tweedale quoted Coates. "There in our own home, and in the presence of fourteen sane and thoughtful people, Mr. Stead has manifested and proved in his own person that the dead do return."

Dr. John S. King, a Toronto physician and president of the Canadian Society Psychical Research, reported receiving over 70 messages from Stead, the first one coming within two days of the *Titanic* disaster. They came through several mediums, including Mrs. Wriedt.

When the *Titanic* went down, Estelle, Stead's daughter, was on a tour with her own Shakespearean Company. One of the members of the touring group was a young man named Pardoe Woodman. According to Estelle Stead, a few days before the disaster, Woodman told her over tea that there was to be a great disaster at sea and that an elderly man very close to her would be among the victims. In 1917, shortly after being discharged from the army, Woodman began receiving messages from William T. Stead by means of automatic writing. Estelle Stead then started sitting with Woodman and observing. She noted that Woodman wrote with his eyes closed and that the writing was very much like her father's. Moreover, the writing would stop at times and go back to dot the "i's" and cross the "t's," a habit of her father's which she was sure Woodman knew nothing about.

Stead informed his daughter that there were hundreds of souls hovering over their floating bodies after the big ship went down, some of them apparently not comprehending their new state as they complained about not being able to save all of their valuables. After what felt like a few minutes, they all seemed to rise vertically into the air at a terrific speed. "I cannot tell how long our journey lasted, nor how far from the Earth we were when arrived, but it was a gloriously beautiful arrival," Stead recorded through Woodman's hand. "It was like walking from your own English winter gloom into the radiance of an Indian sky. There, all was brightness and beauty."

As for his initial attempts to communicate through other mediums, Stead said that there were souls on his side who had the power of sensing people (mediums) who could be used for communication. One such soul helped him find mediums and showed him how to make his presence known. It was explained to him that he had to visualise himself among the people in the flesh and imagine that he was standing there in the flesh with a strong light thrown upon himself. "Hold the visualisation very deliberately and in detail, and keep it fixed upon my mind, that at that moment I was there and they were conscious of it."

He added that the people at one sitting were able to see only his face because he had seen himself as only a face. "I imagined the part they would recognise me by." It was in the same way he was able to get a message through. He stood by the most sensitive person there, concentrated his mind on a short sentence, and repeated it with much emphasis and deliberation until he could hear part of it spoken by the person.

Mike Tymn
Kailua, Hawaii.
December, 2019

A Letter from Sir Arthur Conan Doyle

~

D ear Miss Stead, I found the narrative most interesting and helpful. I have no means of judging the exact conditions under which it was produced or how far subconscious influences may nave been at work, but on the surface of it, speaking as a literary critic, I should say that the clear expression and the happy knack of similes were very characteristic of your father.

We have to face the difficulty that the details of these numerous descriptions of next spheres differ in various manuscripts, but, on the other hand, no one can deny that the resemblances far exceed the differences. We have to remember that the next world is infinitely complex and subdivided – "My Father's house has many mansions" – and that even in this small world, the accounts of two witnesses would never be the same. If a description were given by an Oxford don, and also by an Indian peasant, their respective stories of life in this world would vary much more than any two accounts that I have ever read of the world to come. I have specialised in that direction – the physical phenomena never interested me much – and I can hardly think that anyone has read more accounts, printed, typed and written, than I have done, many of them from people who had no idea what the ordinary Spiritualist scheme of things might be. In some cases the mediums were children. Always there emerges the same idea of a world like ours, a world were all our latent capabilities and all our hidden ambitions have free and untrammelled opportunities. In all there is the same talk of solid ground, of familiar flowers and animals, of congenial occupations – all very different to the vague and uncomfortable heaven of the churches. I confess that I cannot trace in any of these any allusion to a place exactly corresponding to the Blue Island, though the colour blue is, of course, that of healing, and an island may be only an isolated sphere – the antechamber to others.

I believe that such material details as sleep, nourishment, etc., depend upon the exact position of the soul in its evolution, the lower the soul the more material the conditions. It is of enormous importance that the human race should know these things, for it not only takes away all fears of death, but it must, as in the case of your father, be of the very greatest help when one is suddenly called to the other side, and finds oneself at once in known surroundings, sure of one's future, instead of that most unpleasant period of readjustment during which souls have to unlearn what their teachers here have taught and adapt themselves to unfamiliar facts.

Good luck to your little book.

Arthur Conan Doyle,
Crowborough,
Sussex,
England.
September, 1922.

Preface

~

When in April 1912 the *Titanic* sank in mid-ocean and my father passed on to the next world, I was on tour with my own Shakespearean Company. Amongst the members of that Company was a young man named Pardoe Woodman, who on the very Sunday of the disaster foretold it as we sat talking after tea. He did not name the boat or my father, but he got so much that pointed to disaster at sea and the passing on of an elderly man intimately connected with me, that when the sad news came through, we realised he must have been closely in touch with what was about to happen. I mention this incident because it formed the first link between my father and Mr. Woodman, and as it is largely due to Mr. Woodman's psychic powers that my father has been able to get through the messages which are contained in this book. I think, therefore, it will be of interest to readers and should be put on record.

A fortnight after the disaster I saw my father's face and heard his voice just as distinctly as I heard I it when he bade me goodbye before embarking on the *Titanic*. This was at a sitting with Etta Wriedt, the well-known American direct-voice medium. At this sitting, I talked with my father for over twenty minutes. This may seem an amazing assertion to many, but it is a fact vouched for by all those who were present at the sitting. I put it on record at the time in an article published in *Nash's* Magazine, which included the signed testimonies of all those present.

From that day to this I have been in constant touch with my father. I have had many talks with him and communications from him containing very definite proof of his continued presence amongst us. I can truly say that the link between us is even stronger today than in 1912, when he threw off his physical body and passed on the to spirit world. There has never been a feeling of parting, although at first the absence of his physical presence was naturally a source of very great sadness.

In 1917, Mr. Woodman was invalided out of the Army and came to stay with us at our country cottage at Cobham.

Whilst with us, the news came to him that his great friend had been killed at the front, and his interest in the possibility of communication with the next world, which had been indifferent till then, became intense, and he set out to find out for himself. It is ever the passing of a loved one that gives the necessary stimulus for eager inquiry.

It was not long before his friend was able to give him definite proofs of his continued existence and of his ability to communicate. His first proofs were given through Vout Peters and were followed by others through Gladys Osborne Leonard's mediumship and through the mediumship of friends gifted with psychic powers. I was present at that first sitting with Mr. Peters; father was there also, and his friend said it was due to my father's presence and help that he was able to succeed so well in these first attempts at communication.

Shortly after this, Mr. Woodman found that he himself had the power of automatic writing, and father and others were soon able to write through him. Father always prefers me to be present, as if I am not he seems to have more difficulty, and very rarely will attempt writing. He explains the necessity of my presence in this way: he and I are so much en rapport, and so closely in touch with each other, that he is able to draw much power from me; I act as the connecting link and form a sort of battery between him and Mr. Woodman. I merely sit passively by whilst Mr. Woodman Writes. Certainly I see a light around us, and a strong ray of light concentrating on Mr. Woodman's arm.

Sometimes I am able to see father himself, and always, when he is writing, I feel his presence very distinctly.

We have received many messages in this way. For a while in 1918 we sat regularly every week, and were kept in touch with much that was going on at the Front and about what was about to happen, and we were advised of occurrences often days before the news came through in the ordinary way. In one case father gave us the actual headlines which would (and did) appear in the papers the following week.

It is interesting also of importance to note that Mr. Woodman and my father met only once before the passing of latter. I introduced Mr. Woodman to him not long before he left England on the *Titanic*, and they only exchanged two or three words. Therefore, Mr. Woodman never knew my father personally nor has he come into touch with his writings or with his work in any way, and yet the wording and the phrasing of the messages are my father's, and even the manner of writing is typical of him.

Mr. Woodman also writes with his eyes closed and often holds a handkerchief over them. Some of the best messages were given in the twilight when it was impossible for me to follow what was being written, and yet the words were never overwritten. The writing will stop sometimes whilst father evidently reads over what has been written, and alterations will be made, i's dotted and t's crossed correctly.

It was a habit of my father's, whilst here, to go back over his copy and cross his t's and dot his i's; this habit was only known to a few, and was certainly absolutely unknown to Mr. Woodman.

Two of the messages obtained in this way have already been published. They were given by my father for Armistice Day, 1920, and Armistice Day, 1921. For the first, we had no idea he contemplated giving a message. A few friends, including Mr. Woodman, were taking tea with my mother and myself on the Sunday before the 11th of November. We had been chatting on various subjects, when I suddenly felt my father come into the room and could tell by the feeling he gave me that he wished us to give him an opportunity to write, and that it was urgent. It was impossible to arrange for that evening, so we made an appointment for the evening following. Mr. Woodman came about nine o'clock. We sat chatting by the fire for a few minutes; then we felt father come in, and we sat at once.

Father's manner was exactly as it used to be when here in the body and he wanted to get something important done.

He must concentrate on that and on nothing else. Directly we sat, Mr. Woodman's hand began to move, and father wrote words to this effect "I have my message ready, and if you do not interrupt I hope to succeed in getting it through." He wrote at tremendous speed, and in about half an hour had given his message. Having finished, he gave directions that it should be read through and punctuated, if necessary. Then left us, not a word about anything else. It was a strenuous half-hour for us all, but it was worth it.

The message was printed the next day and many thousands distributed to those visiting the Cenotaph that year. The 1921 message was given in the same manner, and thousands of copies of the two messages, now printed in pamphlet form, were distributed on Armistice Day, 1921.

It was soon after giving this last message that father expressed the wish that we should sit for the messages given in this book. We had felt for some time that he was wanting us to sit for a series of messages, but asked that if this were so he would give us definite instructions to this effect from an outside source. This he did by asking Mrs. Kelway-Bamber, the author of "Claude's Books," at a sitting which she was having with Mrs. Leonard, to tell us that it was quite true he did wish us to sit for a series of messages which, he said, would tell of his arrival and some of his experiences on the other side.

Both Mr. Woodman and I are busy people, and can only give what spare time we have from our ordinary work to psychic matters, so that it was difficult to fit in times; therefore it was a few months before we had finished taking the messages. These were all given in the manner already described. They were consecutive, but definite instructions were not given as to how the whole series was to be arranged.

Father's foreword explains his object in writing this book, so there is no need to dwell on that here. When he started, he had a rather longer book in view, but decided in favour of a short book, as it is more likely to be read, can be published at a reasonable price, and so stands the chance of reaching more people. All who worked with my father here will know that such reasoning was characteristic of him.

The photograph given as frontispiece to this volume was taken by the Crewe Circle at Crewe in the autumn of 1915.

In the spring of that year, I had met Mr. Hope and Mrs. Buxton at the house of a mutual friend in Glasgow, and they very kindly invited me to call and see them in Crewe if I should ever have an opportunity to do so. Soon after my return to London father asked me to arrange to go to Crewe, as he said he wanted to try to give us his picture on the same plate with mine. Accordingly I arranged to spend a weekend with some friends at Crewe and have some sittings with Mr. Hope and Mrs. Buxton.

I bought a box of plates in London and took them with me, and I can truthfully say that, that box of plates never left my sight or my possession all the time I was there. I even slept with the box clasped tightly in my hands. We had our first sitting on the Saturday, when I obtained two extras, neither resembling my father. One was of interest because it was the picture of a lady who had appeared on a plate with my father when he was experimenting with Mr. Boursnell in the 'nineties. I took my box containing the rest of the plates away with me after the sitting; bought another box of plates in Crewe, and took both boxes with me to the sitting on the Sunday. We did not use my first box at all at this sitting, and I kept it all the while just inside my dress. We sat around the table, putting our hands over and under the second box for a few minutes; I then held the box for a minute against Mrs. Buxton's forehead. After this I was instructed by Mr. Hope's guide to take the box myself into the dark room (note the box had not been unsealed or the plates exposed to the light). When in the dark room, I was to unseal the box and take out the two bottom plates, taking particular care to note which was the bottom plate, and then to develop both plates. Mr. Hope was to come in with me, but not to touch box or plates. I carried out instructions. I found the bottom plate not even fogged, and on the other plate two messages, one from Archdeacon Colley, deploring father's inability to write; one from Mr. Walker, the father of my host, and in one corner of the plate a faint outline of my father's face. When I got back to my friends that evening, we had a sitting at which father expressed his keen disappointment at his failure to give his picture. "It is all my fault", he said. "I am so excited at the idea of getting my picture beside yours after I have been so-called 'dead' for so many years that I break the conditions; however, many have promised to help me tomorrow, and if I fail again we have something else prepared to slip on so that you will not be quite so disappointed." On the following morning I went for my last sitting. Two of my own plates were used. On both of these are pictures of my father; one is reproduced in this book, the other is a large face of father which completely covers me.

Now, having, I hope, given a little idea as to how these messages were obtained, and our reasons for feeling that they do indeed come from my father, I am content to let The Blue Island do the rest. I am sure it will interest many, and if it awakens some to a truer realisation of what is to come, and makes them seek for further definite proofs themselves, then the three chiefly concerned in giving these messages to the public – my father, Mr. Woodman and myself – will be amply satisfied.

Estelle W. Stead
September, 1922

A Foreword from the Spirit World

~

There is great trepidation on the part of all the uninitiated when first coming into contact with the occult, psychic or unknown forces. In many of life's mysteries there is much pleasure to be had in probing the secret, and the mystery is in itself an incentive to search and to inquire, to overcome the unknown and to gain knowledge on subjects not previously known or proven. This, however, does not seem to apply when dealing with the mysteries surrounding the afterlife. There is always a fear of something. Frequently personal, but sometimes fear of harming the individual known and loved on Earth. In itself that is a good sign; it argues unselfishness, and consequently the individual who holds off for that reason deserves enlightenment. If he is sufficiently advanced to seek, he will get enlightenment together with great help.

Again, there are those who, imbued with theosophical ideas, fear to come in contact with what is to their minds the shell of a former loved one, and those who fear through ignorance due to an undeveloped and somewhat uneducated mentality. By that I do not necessarily mean an unschooled mentality. I speak of "uneducated" in the sense of lacking understanding and appreciation of the higher things of life.

To all these people I am, and I always was, most sympathetic. In earth life I did my best to help and enlighten, but I was very restricted owing to material calls upon my time. Since my arrival in this land I have tried to carry on and greatly to increase the amount and the sphere of this same work. I have succeeded up to a point, though many have not yet reached the halfway step on that staircase of knowledge leading to understanding. I was on the point of saying 'leading to happiness', but that would not be quite correct, for happiness is most amply contained in 'understanding', and happiness in the sense that it is used and understood on Earth is not the raison d'etre of life. We were not made only to be happy. Happiness is part of our reward for work done, for progress and for help given to others – which is itself the outcome of understanding.

As I have said, in my work on this side of the Borderland I have achieved a certain success, and I am confident that if I can pass on the knowledge

I have gained, together with my own personal experiences, to you who are still on Earth, I shall have gone a little farther in the work to which I have set my hand for the good of humanity.

What I have to tell will be of interest to many, and will be useless to many more, but I am going to tell of things which each one of my readers can, up to a point, test for himself.

You can each one of you test it by soul knowledge, and by that you will know that I am giving you words of value, words which God in His infinite love has permitted me to be the means of passing to you. It is not my idea of the mysteries of life; it is a discourse on those mysteries.

There is the teaching of Christianity running all through, but the application is different to that ordinarily accepted.

It is quite erroneous to suppose that because a man was a man on Earth, he will become a spirit angel the moment he dies. Death is only the doorway from one room to another, and both rooms are very similarly furnished and arranged.

That's what I want you to appreciate thoroughly; it is under the same guiding hand. The same personality rules all spheres.

Beginning at the beginning, I have to tell you how a man finds himself here on arrival. As I have said, this whole book will interest many and help a few. It is for that few that all concerned are making the necessary effort to bring it to them. It does not attempt or pretend to be on scientific lines. All through, you can apply sound common sense, and you cannot break down what is.

I have dealt with the subject very briefly, only for the reason that many will read a short, concise account who would not study a detailed one.

I must impress upon you all – the interested and the disinterested, the believer in this great subject, Spiritualism, and the skeptic – to remember you are still on Earth and you have still to perform earth's duties. You have your daily lives to lead and you must always do well the work in hand. Never neglect the present because the future appears more brightly coloured. Carry on with today, but with a corner of your mind on tomorrow, and remember also that phenomenal Spiritualism is not for all. Many minds could not absorb the greatness of the subject together with the facts of the phenomena and still continue in their routine in normal manner – these are the people for whom phenomena Spiritualism is not. They will be wise to go no further into the subject than knowledge gained from books and from the experiences of others. In this sense, Spiritualism is not for all.

William T. Stead.

1

The Arrival

~

Communicated by W.T. Stead
through the hand of Estelle Stead

Experience of a New Arrival Beyond the Veil

Many years ago I was attracted by an article on the subject of spirit communication, and after reading it carefully several times, I was forced to admit its soundness. I was struck by the plain and practical ideas of the writer. This was the first cause of my becoming actively interested in this big and amazing work. From that time onward

I did all in my power to prove and then forward the movement.

Many people know this, and those who do not, can become acquainted with the details if they wish. Therefore I am going to pass at once from my first Earth interest in the occult to my first interest in the Earth.

Just as I was overcome with astonishment and satisfaction on first reaching conviction on Earth, so I was astonished almost equally on my coming to this land and finding that my knowledge of this subject gained on Earth was strikingly correct in nearly all the chief points. There was a great satisfaction in proving this. I was at once amazed and delighted to find so much truth in all I had learned, for although I had believed implicitly, I was not entirely without grave misgivings upon many minor details.

Hence my general satisfaction when I recognised things and features which, though I had accepted whilst on Earth, I had scarcely anticipated would be as I now found them. This must sound somewhat contradictory, but I want you to understand that my earthly misgivings were based on fear that perhaps the spirit world had a formula of its own which was quite different from our earthly mentality, and that, therefore, the many points were transmitted to us in such a form and in such expression as we on Earth would be able to grasp and appreciate, and were not in themselves the precise descriptions, owing to the limitations of earth word-expression.

Of my actual passing from Earth to spirit life, I do not wish to write more than a few lines. I have already spoken of it several times and in several places. The first part of it was naturally an extremely discordant one, but from the time my physical life was ended, there was no longer that sense of struggling with overwhelming odds, but I do not wish to speak of that.

My first surprise came when, although I now understand that to your way of thinking I was dead, I found I was in a position to help people. From being in dire straights myself, to being able to lend a hand to others, was such a sudden transition that I was frankly and blankly surprised.

I was so taken aback that I did not consider the why and the wherefore at all. I was suddenly able to help. I knew not how or why and did not attempt to inquire. There was no analysis then; that came a little later.

I was also surprised to find a number of friends with me; people I knew had passed over years before. That was the first cause of my realising the change had taken place. I knew it suddenly and was a trifle alarmed. Practically instantaneously I found myself looking for myself. Just a moment of agitation, momentary only, and then the full and glorious realisation that all I had learned was true. Oh, how badly I needed a telephone at that moment! I felt I could give the papers some headlines for the evening. That was my first realisation. Then came a helplessness – a reaction – a thought of all my own at home – they didn't know yet.

What would they think of me? Here was I, with my telephone out of working order for the present. I was

3

still so near to the Earth that I could see everything going on there. Where I was I could see the wrecked ship, the people, the whole scene; and that seemed to pull me into action – I could help. And so in a few seconds – though I am now taking a long time to tell you, it was only a few seconds really – I found myself changed from the helpless state to one of action; helpful not helpless – I was helpful, too, I think.

I pass a little now. The end came and it was all finished with. It was like waiting for a liner to sail; we waited until all were aboard. I mean we waited until the disaster was complete. The saved, saved; the dead, alive. Then, in one whole we moved our scene. It was a strange method of travelling for us all, and we were a strange crew, bound for we knew not where. The whole scene was indescribably pathetic. Many, knowing what had occurred, were in agony of doubt as to their people left behind and as to their own future state. What would it hold for them? Would they be taken to see Him? What would their sentence be? Others were almost mental wrecks. They knew nothing; they seemed to be uninterested in everything; their minds were paralyzed. A strange crew indeed, of human souls waiting their ratings in the new land.

A matter of a few minutes in time only and here were hundreds of bodies floating in the water – dead … hundreds of souls carried through the air, alive – very much alive, some were. Many, realising their death had come, were enraged at their own powerlessness to save their valuables. They fought to save what they had on Earth prized so much.

The scene on the boat at the time of the striking was not so pleasant, but it was as nothing to the scene among the poor souls newly thrust out of their bodies, all unwillingly.

It was both heartbreaking and repellant. And thus we waited – waited until all were collected, until all were ready, and then we moved our scene to a different land.

It was a curious journey that. Far more strange than anything I had anticipated. We seemed to rise vertically into the air at terrific speed. As a whole we moved, as if we were on a very large platform, and this was hurled into the air with gigantic strength and speed, yet there was no feeling of insecurity … we were quite steady.

I cannot tell how long our journey lasted, nor how far from the Earth we were when we arrived, but it was a gloriously beautiful arrival. It was like walking from your own Indian Sky. There, all was brightness and beauty. We saw this land far off when we were approaching, and those of us who could understand realised that we were being taken to the place destined for all those people who pass over suddenly – on account of its general appeal. It helps the nerve-racked newcomer to fall into line and regain mental balance very quickly. We arrived feeling, in a sense, proud of ourselves. It was all lightness, brightness. Everything was physical and quite as material in every way as the world we had just finished with.

Our arrival was greeted with welcomes from many old friends and relations who had been dear to each one of us in our earth life. And having arrived, we people who had come over from that ill-fated ship parted company. We were free agents again, though each one of us was in the company of some personal friends who had been over here a long while.

2

The Blue Island

~

I have told you a little about the journey and arrival and I want now to tell you my first impression and a few experiences. I must begin by saying I do not know how long after the collision these experiences took place. It seemed to be a continuation without any break but I cannot be certain that this was so.

I found myself in company with two old friends, one of them my father. He came to be with me, to help and generally show me round. It was like nothing else so much as merely arriving in a foreign country and having a chum to go around with. That was the principal sensation. The scene from which we had so lately come was already well relegated to the past. Having accepted the change of death, all the horror of our late experience had gone. It might have been fifty years ago instead of, perhaps, only last night.

Consequently our pleasure in the new land was not marred by grief at being parted from earth friends. I will not say that none were unhappy, many were, but that was because they did not understand the nearness of the two worlds; they did not know what was possible, but to those who understood the possibilities, it was in a sense the feeling, "Let us enjoy a little of this new land before mailing our news home;" therefore there was little grief on our arrival.

In writing my first experiences I am going to give a certain amount of detail. My old sense of humor is still with me, I am glad to say, and I know that what I have to say now will cause a certain amount of amusement to those who treat this subject lightly, but that I do not mind. I am glad they will find something to smile at – it will make an impression on them that way, and then when their own time comes for the change they will recognise themselves amongst the conditions of which I am going to write.

Therefore to that kind of skeptic I just say, "It's all right, friend," and, "You give no offence." My father and I, with my friend also, set out immediately. A curious thing struck me. I was clothed exactly as I had been, and it seemed a little strange to me to think I had brought my clothing with me! There's number one, Mr. Skeptic! My father was also dressed as I had always known him.

Everything and everybody appeared to be quite normal – quite as on Earth. We went out together and had refreshment at once and naturally that was followed by much discussion about our mutual friends on both sides. I was able to give them news and they gave me information about our friends and also about the conditions ruling in this new country.

Another thing which struck me was the general colouring of the place; of England it would be difficult to say what the impression of colouring is, but I suppose it would be considered grey-green. Here there was no uncertainty about the impression; it is undoubtedly a blue which predominated. A light shade of blue. I do not mean the people, trees, houses, etc., were all blue, but the general impression was that of a blue land.

I commented upon this to my father who, by the way, was considerably more active and younger than he was at time of death; we looked more like brothers. I spoke of this impression of blue, and he explained that it was so in a sense. There was a great predominance of blue rays in the light, and that was why it was so wonderful a place for mental recovery. Now some say, "How completely foolish!" Well, have you not on Earth certain places considered especially good for this or that ailment? Then bring common sense to bear, and realise that the next step after death is only a very little one. You do not go from indifferent manhood to perfect godliness! It is not like that; it is all progress and evolution, and as with people, so with lands. The next world is only a complement of your present one.

We were a quaint population in that country. There were people of all conditions, of all colours, all races and all sizes: all went about freely together, but there was a great sense of caring only for oneself – self-absorption. A bad thing on Earth, but a necessary thing here, both for the general and individual good. There would be no progress or recovery in this land without it. As a result of this absorption there was a general peace amongst these many people, and this peace would not have been attained without this self-centeredness. No one took notice of any other. Each stood for himself, and was almost unaware of all the others.

There were not many people whom I knew.

Most of those who came to meet me had disappeared again, and I saw scarcely any I knew, except my two companions.

I was not sorry for this. It gave me more chance of appreciating all this new scenery before me. There was the sea where we were, and I and my companions went for a long walk together along the shore. It was not like one of your seaside resorts with promenade and band – it was a peaceful and lovely spot. There were some very big buildings on our right, and on our left was the sea. All was light and bright, and again this blue atmosphere was very marked. I do not know how far we went, but we talked incessantly of our new conditions and of my own folk at home and of the possibility of letting them know how it fared with me, and I think we must have gone a long way. If you can imagine what your world would look like if it were compressed into a place, say, the size of England – with some of all people, all climates, all scenery, all buildings, all animals – then you can, perhaps, form an idea of this place I was in. It must all sound very unreal and dreamlike, but believe me, it was only like being in a foreign country and nothing else, except that it was absorbingly interesting.

I want to give you a picture of this new land without going too deeply into the minute details. We arrived at length at a huge building, circular and with a great dome. Its general appearance was of a dome only – on legs – I mean a great dome supported on vast columns, circular and very big. This again, in the interior, was an amazingly lovely blue. It was not a fantastic structure in any way. It was just a beautiful building, as you have on Earth – do not imagine anything fairylike – it was not. This blue was again very predominant, and it gave me a feeling of energy. I wanted immediately to write. I would like to have been a poet at that moment, but as it was I just wanted to express myself with pen and ink.

We stayed there some time and had refreshment very similar; it seemed to me, to what I had always known, only there was no fresh food. Everything appeared quite normal there, too, and the absence of some things which would on Earth have been present was not noticed. The curious thing was that the meal did not seem at all a necessity – it was there, and we all partook of it lightly, but it was more from habit than need. I seemed to draw much more strength and energy out of the atmosphere itself. This I attributed to the colour and air.

It was while we were in this place that my father explained the reason and work of the different buildings I had noted on our walk together.

3

Interesting Buildings

~

Looked upon as a meal – a lunch out – it was the longest one I have ever known and without question the most interesting. I learnt a great deal in those first few hours with my father. It was all conversational but it was of great use to me and of vast interest. He explained to me that the place we were then in was a temporary rest-house, one of many, but the one most used by newly arrived spirit people. It was nearest to earth conditions and was used because it resembled an earth place in appearance. There were other buildings used for the same purpose as well as for other purposes; by that I mean there is more than one of each.

These houses were not all alike, they varied considerably in outward appearance, but there is no need to describe each. To call it a big building is sufficient, and by that you must understand a place like your museum or your portrait gallery, or your large hotels ... anything you like, and it is near enough. But it was not fantastic in any way and had no peculiarities, therefore by "building" I mean a building only.

There were a great number of these places in different parts, not grouped together, but variously placed about this land.

It seems that all the senses are provided for here. The chief work on this island is to get rid of unhappiness at parting from earth ties, and therefore, for the time being the individual is allowed to indulge in most of earth's pleasures.

There are attractions of all kinds to stimulate and generally to tone up strength. Whatever the person's particular interest on Earth has been, he can follow it up and indulge in it here also for the present. All mental interests and almost all physical interests can be continued here, for that one reason of coaxing the newcomer to a level mental outlook.

There are houses given over to book study, music and to athleticism of all kinds. Every kind of physical game can be practiced – you can ride on horseback or you can swim in the sea. You can have all and any kind of sport which does not involve the taking of life. In a minor degree that can be had too, but not in reality; that is only make-believe.

From this you will understand that particular buildings are given over to their own kind of work.

The man who has spent his life in games, heart and soul, would be disconsolate without them here ... he can have them and enjoy them to the full, but he will find that after a time the desire is not so keen and he will turn to other interests automatically, though gradually, and it may be that he will never entirely abandon his games, but the desire will be less absorbing. On the other hand, the man who used his life for, say, music, for instance, will find his desire, his interest, and his ability increasing by leaps and bounds because music belongs to this land. He will find that by spending much time in one of the music houses, as he will if his life is music, his knowledge and ability are amazingly increased.

Then there is the bookworm. He too, finds intense satisfaction in his new found facilities. Knowledge is unlimited – works of priceless value, lost upon Earth, are in existence here. He is provided for.

The keen businessman on Earth whose only interest is in making his business successful will also find scope for ability. He will come in contact with the house of organisation, and he will find himself linked up with work transcending in interest anything that he could have imagined for himself whilst upon Earth.

Now all this is done for a reason. Everyone is provided for. On arriving here there is often much grief; grief that is sometimes incapacitating, and no movement forward can be made until the individual wishes it himself. Progress cannot be forced upon him. Thus, in the scheme of creation the blessed Creator has devised this wonderful means of appealing to the main interest on Earth of each one.

Everyone comes in touch with the chief longing of earth life, and is given opportunity to indulge in it, thus progress is assured.

In all things that are purely and solely of the Earth, the interest flags after a little time; a gradual process – nothing is dramatic here – and the person passes from this to another interest which on Earth would be called a mental one. Those whose interests have been in this mind-category will continue and enlarge the scope of their work, and will progress along the same lines – the others change.

Whilst in this Blue Island each one is very much in touch with the conditions left behind. At first there is nothing done but what is both helpful and comforting – later there is a refining process to be gone through. At first it is possible to be closely in touch with the home left behind, but after a little time, there is a reaction from this desire to be so close to Earth, and when that sets in, the process of eliminating Earth, and flesh instincts begins. In each case this takes a different course, a different length of time.

In trying thus to explain the use of this land and its buildings, I have not numbered them "Building A" for so-and-so, "Building B" for this, that and the other, but, in a conversational way, I hope I have helped you to understand and form a general idea of this country and some of its conditions. I hope I have made it clear now, after a time, the desire for earth things leaves us all. It may be a short or long time, according to the disposition of the person concerned. Take the athlete. He loves his games, his running, his physical strength and his muscular exercise.

Well, he will love it here as much. He will love it here more, because he will find an added pleasure in feeling no fatigue, a sharpened enjoyment altogether, but after a time his appreciation of all this will change. He will not dislike this hitherto loved sport, but he will pass to a different form of it. A form which is full of movement and satisfaction but not a physical affair at all; his mind will become more awake, and he will get enormous mental satisfaction from the studies which will come before him concerning the ways and means of travel here.

Locomotion of all kinds here is very different to that which obtains in earth conditions, and this former athlete of Earth will drop into line in his new surroundings and will presently realise that life here is a different thing for him, for, though still on the same lines, it holds an increased mental interest. Is that clear? Well, apply it in the same fashion to every other type of individual.

4

Life on the Island

~

Having given you a little idea of this land and its appearance, I want to tell you about the life of the people here, so that you can form a mental picture in completeness. It is only natural that many should say, "What are they all doing?" Now, this is a very broad question to answer, and to help you to see how big a thing I am dealing with in thus attempting to give my story of the next life, I must put a simple question to you.

I want you to try to imagine you have not been living on Earth and that, knowing nothing of earth life, you have suddenly been landed by an airship in the busiest part of the city of London – with all its traffic and its people. You have arrived from some other world and have not seen this sight before. You will exclaim, "How strange … what are they all doing?" Well, could you answer that question easily? It would not mean much to you to be told they are going about their own individual business – one man bakes bread, another sweeps the streets, another drives a cart, and another sits in an office and runs a business – all that would leave you none the wiser. These are facts, and yet you would not understand them. You could not comprehend them. That is my difficulty in trying to make you understand in a satisfactory way the life of this Blue Isle. I have to consider how to explain it. It is no use my telling you that one person sits by the sea all the time, weeping because of her parting from her lover, and another is in a mental stupor for drink, and another still thinks he is ringing the bells of his local chapel on Sunday, etc., – that is not the life – those are only bits of it. Atoms of the whole. I do not want to particularise, I want to generalise, with some detail.

Therefore I must say that if you were to pay this land a visit in your Earth bodies, as you are at present, you would be struck by the lack of excitement. You would think it all so like Earth. That is what you would say to people on your return. "Oh, it's so much like our life here, only there are a lot of different races of mankind there." Everyday life for the individual is strikingly like the everyday life he's always been used to. At first he takes a great deal of rest, having the Earth habit of sleep – and it is a necessity – he needs sleep here, too, for the present. We have no night as you have, but he sleeps and rests just the same. He has his interests in visiting different parts, in exploring the land and its building and in studying its animal and vegetable life. He has friends to seek out and to see. He has his pastimes to indulge. He has his newfound desire for knowledge to feed.

The routine of a day here is similar to the routine of a day on Earth; the difference being that Earth's routine is often made by force of circumstance, whereas, here it is made according to desire for knowledge on this or that subject.

In clothing, we are all practically as on Earth, and as there are so many races here you can well understand the general appearance of this land is most unusual, and in an odd way particularly interesting and amusing, also instructive. I think I have said that in general appearance we all are as we all were. We are only a very little way from Earth, and consequently up to this time we have not thrown off Earth ideas. We have gained some new ones, but have as yet discarded few or none.

The process of discarding is a gradual one. As we live here we gain knowledge of many kinds, and come to find so many things, hitherto thought essential, not only of no importance but something of a bore, a nuisance, and that is how we grow to a state of dropping all Earth habits. We get to the state of not desiring a smoke, not because we can't have it, or think it not right, but because the desire for it is not there. As with a smoke, so with food, so with many a dozen things; we are just as satisfied without them. We do not miss them; if we did we should have them, and we do have them until the desire is no longer there.

At first there is practical freedom of thought and action, and there are only certain limitations imposed – not by rule but by conditions. Beyond these limitations there is absolute freedom. After a time, when the spirit has advanced to the point of desiring knowledge and enlightenment, he will be drawn like a piece of steel to a magnet, into contact with this or that house of organisation dealing with the subject on which he desires knowledge.

From the time of coming into touch with this house the spirit will be, as it were, "at school." He will perforce have to attend this house of instruction. He will spend a good deal of his time there learning and when finished with one house, will pass to another, but it is not compulsory information, it is craved-for information, and nothing is given until asked for. You are not forced to acquire anything. You are more than ever free agents. That is why on Earth it is so essential to control your bodies by your minds, and not the reverse. When you come here your mind is all-powerful, and everything depends, for your own degree of happiness here, upon the kind of mind you bring with you.

The presence or absence of contentment is entirely due to the Earth life you have led, the character formed, opportunities taken and lost, the motive of and for your actions, the help given, the manner of help received, your mental outlook and your use and abuse of flesh power. To sum all these up, it is the quality of mind control over body versus body over mind. Mind matters and body matters; it is in your keeping entirely and is in whatever state you have made it by your life. On your arrival here the degree of your happiness will be determined automatically by the demands of your mind.

When you are inclined to ask, "What are they all doing there?" turn your mind to some dear one on Earth who has taken up an out-of-the-way kind of life somewhere abroad, where you are not in constant and intimate touch, and say of him, "I wonder what he's doing now?"... Then answer it yourself by saying "I suppose he's carrying on." So are we, we people in the Blue Island.

5

Intimate Life

~

There is a good deal of reasoning and argument as to why in Earth life we should do this or that. Why we should refrain from many of the delights of everyday life and why we should "go straight." People say it is handicapping their business or their profession to have to observe these "nice points." They may not confess this thought openly, but to themselves they do – they do not see why such-and-such should not be done. True, they think it may injure so-and-so's business a little, but that is his affair.

All in ignorance.

There is a reason, and that reason can be very easily found by the rule of common sense. I almost might call this a discourse upon cause and effect.

Earth life has deteriorated. The whole scheme of creation is planned with great precision, with the object of allowing free individual development and progress. Its rules are laid down clearly. Every man knows by instinct when he is obeying and when disobeying these rules. It needs no police officer to tell him. He may deceive himself that such an act is all that it should be but at the same time he knows in his own consciousness that, that act or thought is not only not all that it should be but that it is all that it ought not to be. I say that all mankind knows – but most of mankind prefers to think it does not know.

Not one person on Earth can stand up and say I am not speaking a profound truth here! Mostly these things are not considered from the point of right or wrong, but from the view, "Shall I benefit by this?" But I say that all people on Earth can discriminate, I do not say that they do, between good and not good motive in their lives. Instinct does this for them. They cannot help themselves. They are bound to know. The trouble is that the vast majority by force of habit, the desire for business gain, or social gain, or any kind of gain, but always a gain for itself, has ceased to consider the quality of its actions and thinks only of the first result. It is a pity.

It is more than that; looked upon from the next stage in evolution it is PITIFUL. Poor undeveloped egos, preparing their own discomfort and suffering – not a hell fire but a mental torture.

The self or spirit of a man is encased in his mind and examined in a purely physical way; the brain is the most baffling organ of the body scientific man ever had to deal with. Much can be understood; all never will be. Judged as being the casing and instrument of the soul it becomes an even more delicate and intricate and baffling piece of work.

You all know that mind is the generating-house for all your acts and deeds, but you do not fully appreciate the fact that every act and every thought is "booked" – is recorded.

You do not see the elaborate scheme of work which goes on in any of your large business houses, when you buy something and do not pay at once. It is booked and passes through many hands before the bill is sent to you a little later, and having paid the bill you forget it all, but the record of that business house has it still. So with the brain; an act or a thought, no matter what the quality, is recorded for all time. Settling will come after life, and when paid the "book" is finished with and troubles no more, though the record is still there. Now follow me. Mind and its work – thought – is the force that drives and creates everything on Earth. It has all to be mental before physical or material. That you all know. Every building was conceived mentally before being built.

Thought is divided in itself into different types. There is the thought of your next meal which is of no particular interest, and there are the thoughts constructive and destructive. These are important. There are the purely personal thoughts. Sometimes advantageous and sometimes the reverse. Now, the all-important forms of thought are the constructive and destructive. The others referring to your meals, your clothes, your appearance, your anything you like, these are not of importance until they are allowed to hinder the flow of constructive thought; when they do this the character of these same thoughts changes and becomes destructive.

It is the material embodiment of destructive thought which causes most of the distress and misery in the world.

The sum total goes on increasing, and will continue to increase, until mankind as a whole, and individually, will listen and try to understand a little more about himself beyond what is necessary for him to know for the selling of his goods, and thus give fuller play to the beneficent action of constructive thought which alone can redeem and save the world.

6

Intimate Life (continued)

~

To a great extent the individual hardships of Earth life are directly due to wrong thinking. I am fully aware that people are placed in many different positions right from birth.

Some inherit unhappiness and difficulty from their parents, and their lot in life is harder and their pleasures are less than in the lives of those who are born in better conditions.

Accepting these differences of position and condition – one man a life of much hard work, another a comfortable and perhaps rather idle life – the same rule of thought applies. The man who has grown up under hard conditions is by circumstances forced into a groove of thought – a regular rut. He cannot help himself because there are no real attempts made by any to change his outlook; he may meet with material help from time to time, but he meets with little practical mental assistance. He is under the disadvantage of his lifelong Earth conditions, and is in ignorance because he does not understand and has little opportunity for learning about these things. By his thought he adds to his difficulties instead of easing and finally removing many of them. The other man, who is comfortably settled and has no particular worries, does precisely the same thing. He trudges along in the same mental rut – stagnation, *mental stagnation*, and the same results will fall to them both hereafter. They are both building up their future states.

Then there are people of keen intelligence, clever people, who use their brains to achieve material gain no matter the cost to others. These people are indulging in the most positive form of destructive thought. They are not like the other two – negative.

They are very alive, alert and positive. They are at once using destructive and constructive thought. The latter is entirely misapplied, and when they come here the account against them will be much heavier, because they will have built up a wall of greedy thought which themselves have originally sent out and which they must settle in this next condition.

A thought, no matter the heading it comes under, that has come into your mind and which you have sent out is an accomplished thing so far as your mind goes. Your physical act may or may not keep swift accompaniment with the thought; that does not matter from the point of view of what you are building up for yourself here. Once having had his thought it is done, so far as your mind is concerned, and, whether you follow it up actively or not, you have to make repayment for it when you come here. I am not speaking about the thousand trivial thoughts of every hour, but about those which I might describe as having personality.

You will say it is impossible to control every thought of the day, and I agree that it is, but if once you accepted for fact what I have said you would keep a sharp eye on your mental actions. They matter. You will find this very difficult to accept because it is indeed an intimate thing for each one; you do not know each other's thoughts whilst upon Earth, therefore I have headed this chapter "Intimate Life." Each of you will live to thank the person who is responsible for giving you this information if you act upon it, and those of you who hear and know but do not act upon the knowledge, will have one day to cast reproaches upon yourselves for this failure.

To realise oneself that one has failed is far more bitter than the consciousness that others know it.

Think upon this and reason a little with your own inner self.

7

First Attempts

~

L eaving the question of time out of it entirely, as I must, I want to write of my first attempt to communicate with the Earth world. I know there is much dissatisfaction with the spirit world on account of the practical impossibility to give correct ideas of time-spacing. I would like to say a little about that before going into the main interest of today's writing. You must not be over-hasty in condemning us for this failure. On Earth you all space your time by days and hours, etc., but those spacings are also based, or perhaps more definitely marked in your mental reckoning, on the habits of the day. You have always taken certain things at certain hours. You have a light sky and a dark sky; without a watch you know fairly accurately the time of day by your inclinations – fatigue or freshness, the need for food or rest, etc., etc.

Now, on this side of the grave we have no real necessity for rest or for food. We have no dark sky – only a light one, and we have, for the sake of the present illustration, an unlimited supply of energy.

Consequently we are not able to break up time into spaces which correspond with earth-spacings. We do break up our time, but it is not your breaking, therefore we can seldom be accurate in telling when a thing did, or when a thing will, happen. For that reason I am not able to tell how long I had been in this country before I made my first attempt to link up with Earth again. To me I seemed to have lived in this land always. It appeared incredible to me that it could be only a few days since I arrived. I had not forgotten my family or my friends, but I felt peculiarly happy about them. I cannot think why, except that finding my Earth knowledge so very correct I gathered strength in feeling that they too would understand everything was quite well with me, and that this little delay in writing was natural considering the new country I had come to.

The house which is given over to this work in the Blue Island had been a regular haunting-place of mine ever since my father had told me of it, together with the works of the other buildings. I went to this house a great deal, and received much help from the various people in charge. They were all very sympathetic, but entirely business-like. It was not merely a house of tears and sympathy, it was an amazingly well organised and business-like place. There were many hundreds of people there. Those who had on Earth believed and those who had not, came to try to wire a message home.

The heart call was the one which received the most serious attention. Many were there only as lookers-on, incredulous and facetious. They got nothing more than the satisfaction of their own amazement.

After a little time my turn came.

For a building given over to this kind of work it appeared to be inadequately equipped. I had rather expected to see many implements and instruments, many wires and machines, and the presence of electric forces, but there was nothing of that kind at all. It was all and only the human element.

I had a long conversation with a man there – a man obviously of some importance, though I cannot say he looked like an angel; he appeared quite as mundane as myself.

I had a long talk with him, and from him heard how a great deal of this work was carried on. He told me they had a system of travellers, whose work was very close to physical Earth. They had the power of sensing people who could and would be used for this work at the other end. These men could locate and then tabulate the Earth people, marking each individual ability, and when the newly arrived spirit came in search of help, these sensitives on Earth were used as each could be used.

This is a sketchy outline of the work done in that building … There I came frequently and tried to get my messages through to home by more than one means; I succeeded in some ways, I failed in others. The spirit has much to do himself with the success or failure attained; a great deal depends upon him. Every time I succeeded I helped another. Every time I failed I went for help, and got it. Having given much time and study to the subject on Earth, I was given unlimited assistance at this end of the line now that I needed it.

I want to explain how I got some of my first messages through and how I knew I had succeeded. We had been taught by this time how to come in close contact with the Earth, although it was not possible for me to do this alone. I had a helper with me. I must call him an official. He came with me to my first trial.

We came into a room, which seemed to have walls made of muslin – something and yet nothing. I know it was a house, and was conscious of the walls of the room, and yet they seemed such poor things because we could see through them and move through them. I could not have done this by myself at that time, but with my official we did.

Then came the attempt. There were two or three people in this room and they were all talking together about the horror of this great disaster and about the probability of people coming back. They were holding a séance, and my official showed we how to make my presence known. The controlling force, he told me, was thought. I had to visualise myself among these people in the flesh. Imagine I was standing there in the flesh, in the center of them, and then imagine myself still there with a strong light thrown upon me; create the picture. Hold the visualisation very deliberately and in detail, and keep it fixed upon my mind, that at that moment I was there and that they were conscious of it. I failed, of course, at first, but I know that after a few attempts I succeeded and those people did actually see me. My face only, but that was because in my picture I had seen myself only as a face. I imagined the part they would recognise me by. I was also able to get a message in the same way; precisely the same way. I stood by the most sensitive present, and spoke and concentrated my mind on a short sentence, and repeated it with much emphasis and deliberation until I could hear part of it spoken by this person. I knew that at last I had succeeded, and I succeeded reasonably easily because I knew so intimately what the conditions of those people and that Earth room were. Many who had not my Earth knowledge made little impression at all.

There was none of my own family present that time. Had there been it would have made it impossible for me, as I was then feeling their sorrow acutely, and I would not have been able to give my mind so full a power as I did – I became almost impersonal. It was a good thing that my first attempt was purely a test one – to see if I could break through to home.

8

The Reality of
Thought Communication

~

In trying to establish a definite form of communication between the Earth sphere and the Blue Island, people are always looking for the return of the physical part of the individual. They find it exceedingly difficult to accept even the most pressing mental tests as being proof of communication, and in giving so much attention to this physical form, they nearly overlook the form of thought communication, which is much more personal and very much less tainted by outside influence, such as the medium's mind, or other sitters antagonism, or bias either way. This thought communication is a much more real form than is accepted by the majority of believers in the possibility of it.

In concentrating the mind on any one spirit person, you are sending out real, live, active forces. These forces pass through the air in precisely the same way as electric waves do, and they never miss their mark. You concentrate on Mr. A in the spirit world, and immediately Mr. A is conscious of a force coming to him. In this land we are much more sensitive than whilst on Earth, and when thoughts are directed to us by people on your side, we have a direct call from those currents of thought thus generated, and we are practically always able to come in close contact with the person who is thinking of us; when near and acclimatised to his conditions we can impress thoughts and ideas upon his mind. He will seldom accept them for what they are, but will think they are his own normal thoughts or something of a hallucination. Nevertheless, if frequent opportunity is given he will be startled at the amount of information he can record. This applies to everyone, not merely to the believer in these subjects. Anyone who sits for a moment and allows his mind to dwell on some dear one who had "died" will actually draw the spirit of that person's to himself. He may be conscious or unconscious of the presence, but the presence is there.

If people on Earth realised the result of their thoughts upon those to whom they refer, they would be very much more careful in giving their mind free play. There are so many thoughts possible, and all of them are registered here; many of them affect the people they concern, but all of them affect the people from whom they emanate.

Perhaps in telling you all thoughts are recorded I am making it more difficult for you to accept and understand.

It will be better, therefore, to explain that by "all thoughts" I refer only to all "direct" thoughts. In reality every thought is registered; the personal ones are, as I have previously said, of no importance so long as they are not allowed to grow into destructive thoughts.

In speaking of direct thought I mean you to understand positive thoughts, about other people, pleasant or unpleasant, and not the thoughts of every day trivialities.

Many people find it impossible to believe that every direct thought they have is registered, or that it can in any way influence or affect the person concerned, or return to influence themselves, but this is so.

You are fully aware of the influence given out by any one person who is deeply depressed or more than usually excited and happy. Each of you has felt this influence. This is, of course, caused by the lowered or raised mental vibrations, giving out particularly strong currents of either depression or happiness.

They are equally strong currents in themselves although they act differently upon the people with whom they come into contact. It is in this way that all direct thoughts act.

Frequently the subject is not conscious of these thoughts upon himself, but influence is there in a subtle and greater or lesser degree of strength, and all these thoughts are very definitely registered in the mind of the thinker long after the incident itself has passed.

When coming to this land, that whole record has to be dealt with. Not by a judge in wig and gown, but by our own spirit selves. In spirit life we have a full and clear remembrance of all these things and, according to quality of these individual thoughts, so we are brought into a state of regret, happiness or unhappiness, despair or satisfaction. It is here that we meet with the desire to make return, to put right all the discomfort and distress, minor or major, as it may be, caused by thoughtless mind action whilst on Earth.

This is why I say that whilst on Earth it is not only advisable, but essential to keep your minds under control and in order. It is only wisdom so to do. The difficulty is that people will not realise this whilst upon Earth, although they know from their own inner consciousness that I am stating a truth.

I want you all to try to realise the results you are making, the unhappiness you are causing others, and the regret and sorrow you are laying up for yourselves in the next world when you have to face the conditions you have made.

Remember that your minds are the generating-houses. You are building up whatever is to be your next condition, precisely and exactly by the lives you are leading on Earth, by your thoughts and by the degree to which your body controls your mind instead of your mind ruling supreme. So long as you are upon Earth you are Body (Physical) and Soul (Mind) and Spirit (Self). When you come here you are Mind (Soul) and Self (Spirit) only. Therefore for your own future happiness it is essential that your Mind should rule during Earth life. It is for you to say whether it shall do so. If you are willing to pay your bill when you come over, carry on as you are, but there is no further credit given; you have to settle it here. If you are a quarter as practical as you each and all think you are, you will see to it that the mind leads. It can lead very delightfully, although you may think it leads only to religious restriction – it does not only lead there; it leads to all Earth's pleasures, all Earth's enjoyments, but it always holds the ruling hand, and can stop at the right time, whereas the body cannot, and so it runs up debts which have to be paid, and paid sometimes very dearly and bitterly.

Earth was made beautiful for Man to enjoy – not merely to tantalise him – lead him on and then say, "No." That is not the way of our blessed Creator. He has given beauty and the faculty for enjoying beauty to all mankind, and so long as the mind rules it will continue to be beauty, but when only the body rules, influencing and degrading the mind as it will, then trouble lies ahead; much trouble and much acute regret.

When we are here our minds work in the same manner, they obey the same rules, and the presence or absence of body does not hinder our thinking powers, and consequently there is no difficulty in coming into touch with some of our people left behind and being

43

in close touch with them, influencing them greatly, although many of them are unconscious of it. I want you to think of this and to realise that your own people can come to you, that thought is all-powerful and that you can build up or destroy, help or hinder, draw near you, or drive away from you, the people incarnate and discarnate, who were and who are so dear to each of you by this power of thought.

Thought communication is the closest link between the two worlds, but it must be well-ordered and well-trained brain action. You must not imagine that every idea which enters your mind is put there by a spirit person; it is not so at all, but at the same time, if you train your mind in the way an athlete trains his body, you can then ask for and receive great knowledge and much help, both spiritual and material.

9

Important Points

~

Asubject of this importance and interest is full of queries. Each one has his own questions to put, and each brings what he considers a hitherto unnoticed point. I want, if possible, to answer a few of these constantly recurring queries now. I had many put to me during my investigations whilst on Earth, and some of them I can answer at last. I want you first to realise that by the change of death you do not become part of the Godhead immediately. The mysteries of life of life are not revealed to you as a kind of welcoming gift on your arrival here. You must not think that I, or any, have full knowledge on all subjects, profound and trivial, the moment we come to spirit life. I cannot tell you when your grandson will next require new shoes ... nor can I tell you the settlement of the Irish question. I can only see a little farther than you, and I do not by any means possess the key to the door of All Knowledge and All Truth. That, we have each to work for … and as we pass through one door we find another in front of us to be unlocked … and another and another.

But, on the other hand, remember that I do know considerably more than you do, because I am in more intimate touch with the main source of knowledge, and I have passed through an experience which is still ahead of you all.

I should like first to speak about the word "conditions" and its true meaning. It is a word which is grossly misapplied in all forms of psychic work. It is given as a reason for this or that failure – for a success – for any peculiarity in result, and it is looked upon as necessary in any apartment in which a meeting is to be held. Rightly and wrongly – usually wrongly. The main factor or essential in obtaining good results lies in the condition of the sitter's mind more than in the room he is in. The mental attitude and the physical state of the sitter is of very much more importance than of the presence of draped windows, thick carpets, exotic perfumes, etc., etc. It is the method of mental approach which matters chiefly. That is a feature often overlooked by even first-grade sensitives. Certain "extras" if rightly used and properly directed round the apartment, such as a cheerful face, pleasant flowers, laughter and brightness, these are all quite useful assets, but they are not the essentials.

Some people always try to reduce to ridicule communication with the next world, one of the greatest of God's blessings to mankind, and complain of what they consider to be the senseless conditions ruling at a séance.

Many of these conditions, as I have said, are meaningless and sometimes a hindrance, but at the same time others are necessary according to the kind of communication sought after.

To make my point, I must recall to you how conditions govern everything, and so much does everything depend upon given suitable conditions that people do not even notice that this is so. The simplest and perhaps the most useful example of this is in making a pot of tea. You must have the tea in a certain condition, you must have the water in a certain condition – if you do not, you get poor results.

Your flowers – you have your seeds in a certain condition of dryness and you put them to Earth when the climate is in a certain condition, according to time of year, and, once planted, you tend your plants, flowers, trees, everything according to the conditions they demand. We demand conditions. Why should you think that this great scientific work can be governed, mastered by inexperienced hands at any take-it-or-leave-it moment? You cannot reasonably expect it, and if you do, you won't get it! Conditions govern Earth and all forms of life on it, from an earlier state than that when consciousness begins – but I tell you many of the conditions demanded by intelligent workers in this subject are futile and – worse – harmful.

You cannot achieve success in anything, or along any line, by directing your force in opposition to your intelligence. A vast number do, in this subject, and that is why there is so much failure.

You may as well try to take a photograph without putting any film into the camera, and, because you get no result, say the whole thing is impossible and fraudulent. You must have conditions in order to secure success in any and everything. It is due to lack of these necessary conditions that we fail sometimes to influence a person to do or not to do a certain act. A father in spirit life may be fully conscious of his son contemplating a certain deed, say, suicide or murder, or anything of that kind. Such knowledge will cause great sorrow to the father, and he will work his utmost to influence the son, to direct his thoughts, and destroy the idea of whatever is contemplated, but at such time the son is in an abnormal state of excitement, which nearly always prevents our influence from getting to him and working upon him. It is not at all a state of happiness, for the father, because he is fully aware of his son's acts, and he is powerless to prevent him.

In action we are free – absolutely free. We have graduated in the Blue School. We are free to go amongst the other spheres. The hands where many or several – or none – of our own people are. We can go to them and we can take help from those more developed, and give help to those less fortunate. Help by advice, help by demonstration, and help by association. We are still living on the Blue Island; not yet do we pass to the next sphere for domicile.

As we are able to travel among these other lands, so we are able to be in constant touch with Earth. Thoughts of us sent out by people on Earth reach us, and we sense from whom they come, and can follow up the person, if so desired. We would not get every thought from anyone who happened to see our names and make a casual remark, but from anyone with whom we were intimate whilst on Earth a thought of us will come straight, as along a telephone wire from one house to another, and if we wish we can come. In this way we are able to help people left behind. We can follow their actions and their minds, and influence them one way or the other, according to our idea of what is for their good; but we cannot do impossible things even for those dearest to us.

Whilst on Earth one can give advice, but one cannot force it into practice – so here we can influence but not create.

Having attained this state there is no parting, there is no sting to death, we can be with our own beyond us, with us, below us, and with those still on Earth. Separation and partings are not known except by the law of attraction and affection. We leave people behind on the Earth who dutifully mourn for us, who are genuinely upset at their loss; but after a while – short or long – their remembrance of us grows thin. They cease to think of us, to recall us, and to remember our companionship. They are the only partings. In some cases even those people come back to our lives when they themselves come to this land. Gradually, as they throw off the influences which dimmed their remembrance of us, they find the foundation of the old affection. Sometimes it is untouched; sometimes spoilt; but these are the only partings.

A spirit who comes here, and is anxious to get in touch with Earth ties, may be made more unhappy by being with the Earth people, for if they do not understand that he is still alive, they are all sadness, and they think of him as dead – as something finished. Although the spirit will go to them a great deal at first, the Earth people will not know he is there, and seeing them but being unable to make his presence know causes him much disappointment and sorrow, and they are ignorant of his presence and think only of him as dead, he will finally stay away altogether, content to wait until they join him. This accounts for many people who are not apparently making any attempt to communicate, and for Earth people to say that this cannot be true because their dearest so-and-so never made any sign to them.

When you are over in this life you will not be continually associated with people who are not of interest to you. On Earth you eliminate, as far as practicable, the people who tire and try you – but here that can be done effectively because those feelings and instincts are entirely mutual. The governing force is love.

Affections bind people together, and if the love between any two, or any group, is a strong and real thing, then those people are in close unison and happiness together. But wherever the love is not on both or all sides, there is automatically a falling away of the affected party. Nothing uneven or unequal holds. When you come, through death, you are attracted by the ties of love into the set of people who vibrate the same affection, and if you have had an affection for another which is not equally shared although you will at first be together, you will gradually and yet quietly cease to attract each other, and cease to be in each other's company.

10

The State of Freedom

~

Everything is ordered. I have touched lightly upon my first arrival and my impression of the new surroundings, and of my first return to Earth and the manner of it.

Without giving technical and scientific formula at all, I think I have given you a fair picture and a rough idea of the next step after Earth life. What I have said applies to all the human race; white, black and yellow – there is no differentiation; one rule holds for all races of mankind.

I shall pass for the present to a further stage.

I may return to say more about the Blue Island, but now I will leave all life there to continue on its way, and will deal with a further point of development – the state of being rid of most Earth instincts. Once rid of these we are able to pass with comparative ease, and almost at will, from one sphere to another, and from this or another sphere back to Earth; keeping thereby in close association with our own people – or those of them who desire it.

We help by influencing them in their daily lives and actions, and we do this without in any way retarding our own work, development and construction of character.

Character is the main thing to be studied.

Whilst on the Blue Island I studied, as all do, the secrets of self and of life, and I came to realise the vastness of Creation. It is not life on Earth and then life on this island only. As progress is made and Earth's inclinations and habits are put aside, so other interests take their place, and then comes the desire for true knowledge. As other do and will do, so did I. I fell into line also and as I learned so I progressed. Capacity for wisdom grew with the wisdom acquired.

I had learnt of the existence of other lands besides this island, and at one time it seemed as incredible as the possible existence of this land does to many now on Earth, but eventually the time came when I was taken to these other spheres. I cannot tell where they are, but it was like traveling amongst the stars. It seems as if we left our world and traveled through space until we reached another star, another land.

There are several of these other lands, and they are inhabited by former Earth people who have progressed sufficiently to qualify for entry into this or that land. These other lands are nearly all inhabited by a higher form of life, a happier form and individually, a more powerful form, but there are one or two other lands of not so high an order, where happiness is less or not at all, according to whether life on Earth was a well or lightly ordered thing. In these lands the people who are there fail and fail again to find the spirit in themselves to desire to rise, to improve and control themselves, although the necessary strength is offered and offered and even thrust at them.

All races have the gift of free will. All are free agents in determining their own destinies. At all times, not only after the body's death. Just as a father and a mother of a family order the day's routine for their children, and allow the children then to amuse themselves in their own way, so the races of mankind are free to develop and model their lives upon their own individual pattern – being given certain rules to conform to. All life is originally free, but whilst on Earth, through poor comprehension and mismanagement, the individual often thinks he is not a free personage with free will – but he is. As the same father and mother will influence and guide their children, the cause being love, so when we are here and find ourselves able, we do our utmost to help and influence those we love who are still on Earth.

Always it is the driving force of love which causes us to do our work.

We can be in close touch with our people on Earth, and by suggestion and by close association we can influence them. Through our influence often much material good will come to them. We spirit people cannot give material riches to any on Earth, but we can frequently advise as to the best step to take in a business matter which, if taken, will bring in considerable material wealth. Just as we can influence in a spiritual sense, so we can influence in a business way. We people over here can see both sides of the argument. When a thing is to be decided between two people we can see both points and can therefore see which is right, and if we play straight we throw our influence in with that, whether it is to the benefit of our Earth friend, in a material sense, or not. If we do this, and our Earth friend loses or suffers from it, we invariably make it up later in a different way. If we throw our influence against our own conviction, only in order to help our Earth friend, we pay for it here ourselves, and our Earth friend, who thereby gains unjustifiably, pays for it later, either whilst on Earth or when in spirit life. He will have to make return sooner or later; there is no escape, it is automatic.

In saying we can and do influence people on Earth, I do not propose to go into the precise process of how we work. It is near enough to say that you know how you influence each other on Earth; here the result is the same, although the process is quite different – but that is a matter which each one of you will deal with individually later on, when your own change comes, therefore it is not of necessity nor of interest to you to know now.

You have on Earth a saying that "coming events cast their shadows before." This is a truth. They do cast their influences, and sensitive people can always register them and can often make a guess at their origin.

11

Premonitions

~

There are many superstitions and many reasons given to explain what is called "premonition," but in almost every instance it can be traced to telepathy; there are so many forms of mental sympathy.

The chief form of premonition is that concerning the death of another – a friend or relation. Now, that can always be traced to telepathy. You will argue that perhaps the person about to pass on was not anticipating his death. It may have been through a sudden accident, and yet so-and-so had a certain sign – a premonition – so many days, or such and such a time, beforehand.

To explain: Mr. A has a premonition about the death of Mr. B. It is followed up later by an accident in which Mr. B is killed. The spirit friends who are interested in Mr. B have been in continual attendance upon him, and are watching him in order to be of use whenever possible; but they cannot make him do this or do that with any certainty, they can only influence him one way or another. Now, all the actions of Mr. B's life are producing certain effects, some of which Mr. B himself is not at once conscious of. His spirit friends are, and they can see, a certain distance ahead, what the results of these actions, the general routine of his life, may be. In this way they can see ahead what is going to occur to Mr. B, and although they will do their utmost to guide him, they cannot act for him. He sets his own destiny in motion and he alone can alter it. At such a time, the spirit friends, realising that Mr. B is in physical danger, will do their utmost to divert his actions and movements: sometimes they are successful, but in this particular instance they are not, and Mr. B meets his death. The influences being used by the spirit people have created a disturbance of thought force around him and, although he was not conscious of it himself, his friend Mr. A has registered it upon his mind and it has reproduced itself in sleep, as a dream, or as a vision built up by thought-power and materialised through and from the physical strength of Mr. B. Distance between A and B makes no difference.

Premonitions concerning an arrangement made which is afterwards not fulfilled are caused by the influence of spirit friends trying always to guide their charges to the benefit of themselves. In this way you can figure out the cause of all so-called premonitions. In every case it is spirit friends trying to communicate with the person chiefly concerned – he often fails to register what another will pick up.

12

Residence

~

I come now to the last days on the Blue Island and the taking up of our residence on the next and far more permanent world. The Blue Island is a transient life; a land for acclimatising the newcomer, and as soon as he's fit he passes from it to what I might term the Real World, inasmuch as each one will be much longer on it than any has yet been on Earth. We can at will return to the Blue Island, and many do so frequently, both to meet newly arrived friends and associates, and to help any person or group with whom we are in sympathy. These are only visits, and we do not ever again return there to live.

Travel here is a very different thing to the methods you all know, and we all set out in a large party for the Real World. Not our whole party, as on first arrival;

many weren't ready to leave, but with us were many other spirit people besides those with whom we had originally arrived.

There was the same sensation of flying, moving rapidly through the air; then we came to our new home. After the colour and generally striking appearance of the Blue Island, this new land appeared less attractive at the outset. It was more toneless in colour, the people more engrossed in their regular routine. It seemed as if we had returned to Earth life again, it was so like. I think, on arrival here, we must all have been attracted to different parts of this land, for my own seemed strikingly like parts I had known on Earth, and there were also buildings I knew.

Other people have told me the same, so I am confident that according to our race and degree of development so we are automatically attracted to different parts of this new world.

It is in this land that I and most of our people are, and certainly all will be, in due course. We continue our studies and our work of developing spiritually, whilst at the same time controlling and dispersing the few still-clinging Earth habits and thoughts. We are all very much more conscious of each other in this land, and life resumes a much greater similarity to the life we have known on Earth. We have our homes in the same way and our interests in other people, and according to taste so we are habited together in houses or on the open hillside country.

Some people live in very elaborate palaces, and it is very curious to note that many of these people are those who have led very rough and hard lives upon Earth. Their idea of Heaven is a palace and a life of ease. After a period of time, during which they must make specified progress in general development, these people are given their palaces in order to allow them full advantage of environment to make forward steps in their evolution. If they don't progress, they lose their palace and must requalify for it. This applies to everyone; each has to qualify in order to obtain his desired object; and in order to keep it he must continue his progress and his help to others.

When we come to this land, we have ceased to desire food, drink and sleep; we are now pure spirit in the rough state; there is still more refining to be done in the next phase. Here, also there are rest houses – houses for music – houses for scientific research – houses for all, and every kind of information and knowledge; and the entrance fee to each and all of these is "desire." We do not lead a life of continual cramming of information – we lead ordinary Earth lives, but with a much keener social interest and much more freedom and exchange of thought. There is no distinction of the classes. Our Earth life may be forgotten, in so far as our individual task on Earth is concerned, when that task was a matter of little or no interest to us. It is only the spiritual and mental knowledge and development which hinders and advances the individual here, and spirit knowledge is not hindered by whatever one's job on Earth may have been. In this respect there is a great and sudden broadening of the point of view of all comers to this land.

It is a land of freedom – a land of happiness and smiles. A land of happiness brought about through the real love of man for man. A land to work for – a land in which your place is made according to the knowledge you have had whilst upon Earth and the way you have used that knowledge.

It is impossible to over-emphasise the degree of freedom in this new world, or the joy each and all has in it.

In saying that your happiness is gauged by the knowledge acquired on Earth and the application of that knowledge, I am saying what is accurate to the smallest detail, but I would like to explain precisely.

On being established here, in the Real World, each one is interviewed by one of the advanced spirit instructors and the whole record of Earth is discussed and analyzed.

Reason, motive and result. The full and detailed record contains everything; there is nothing overlooked, and this is the time for paying the bill. Each is interviewed alone, and there is a minute analysis of all events, acts and thoughts.

Then there is the making good to be gone through, the sum total to be paid … for all our thoughtlessness and our unkind acts and words – all that have had direct results must be paid for.

We have then to spend time in close touch with Earth, in order, by influence, to make good for our past misdoings; make good as far as possible. Also we have the knowledge and full sight of the results of these earlier acts, and they do not bring happiness; but after that state is passed and we can bring all these things into proper perspective and form a table of work, which will gradually and continually be working out results and troubles we have caused, then we can each one settle down to live here in freedom.

The form of life differs here enormously according to temperament, personality, and the influence of Earth life. People vary in strange contrast to one another. Many of us carry on with our same work as on Earth. Here we have no need to work in order to obtain daily livelihood – we work here solely for spiritual refinement and progress – at the same time we keep in touch with our Earth interests as a form of recreation.

We are not always, without any break, in one house or another studying this, that and the other – we have a certain program to go through but it has many breaks, and in this "off duty" time we come back to our dear people on Earth, and either out of interest and love, or from the desire to be useful, we try our utmost to help them in their material and mental difficulties.

We have every form of recreation here, as I have already told you when dealing with the Blue Island. Any habit or hobby formed on Earth can be indulged in here, always providing it is progressive.

From this you can understand that life after death is a very normal and natural affair. We have still our affections, and those which last are still strongly binding links.

Between families and friends we have the same affections – and yet not the same, because sometimes on Earth there are differences which cause a silence between members of a family, and perhaps over here that family will once more be very united – the earth differences being based solely upon material things – once remove the material and physical and underneath the love often remains.

One great change which death brings is a much broader point of view and a much larger mind. A deeper understanding, a keener intuition, clears away immediately many former difficulties and misunderstandings. Once in this Real World, and once past the first initiation and payment of debts, we are free to do as we wish, but we have to progress or we ourselves curtail our liberties. It is not an enforced progress; we can take our own time about everything, but we must not allow any of Earth's instincts to increase in their power over us. We have to learn the new conditions and live for them entirely.

Once free, we can travel at will over our own world and yours. So great is our speed and method of travel that we can be in two places almost simultaneously.

Everywhere we go we are conscious of the general love for one another. It is much more evident than on Earth, and that great affection is the direct cause of the general brightness and radiance of this world. I do mean that it gives off rays of light, but rather that the general atmosphere is light in quality and very invigorating and strength-giving.

Life here is a grander thing – a bolder thing, and a happier thing for all those who have led reasonable lives on Earth, but for the unreasonable there are many troubles and difficulties and sorrows to be encountered. There is a great truth in the saying that "as ye sow, so shall ye reap."

13

General Results

~

I have been away from my Earth life now a number of years, and although I have been in constant and unbroken touch with my old conditions and affections, I have never, since leaving the Blue Island, had any desire to return to the Earth for habitation.

There have been many occasions when I have very badly wanted a tongue for a few hours. With my extra sight I have known the right treatment when seeing certain situations being mishandled. At such times I have very badly wanted to return to Earth for an hour, in order to be the means of bringing about great improvements – beyond these passing desires I have had no wish ever to take up residence on Earth; my travels and my works and studies on this side of the grave have been of such vital interest. Since being here I have acquired greater knowledge, and have been able to pass to Earth people some of that knowledge, at different times. Ever since my leaving the world – your world – I have been keenly interested in its development, and very live to all its internal and external difficulties. Patriotism still holds with me, as with most of us, and will continue to hold so long as I have personal ties upon Earth. When there are no longer any of these personal ties remaining, my interests will gradually and naturally turn more exclusively to this side among my own people, and my place will be filled by another – and so the race goes on – always moving forward, progressing and evolving.

Looking back on it all since I first came to the Blue Isle I have great satisfaction in seeing the advance I have made.

Coming here was quite a shock to me. I had no idea that my death was so near when that particular year began, and I certainly had no desire that it should be soon. I had an overwhelming number of important things on my hands.

Some of these have been able to finish since, and I have followed the progress of many others. Soon after arrival, I had grown acclimatised to the new conditions, the new appearance of everything, the new power of locomotion and communication. We do not talk to each other very much here, we have a more expressive and intimate way than that. Here, thoughts are communicated from one mind to another without the need of vocal expression, although we can talk in earth manner at will.

There are, of course, many and vast differences between my world and yours, but I always find one of the most blessed and merciful differences between the two to be the manner in which the mental is unhindered by the physical.

You on Earth have mental desires and ambitions of various kinds; for money, success in business, pleasure, power, knowledge, etc., but always these desires are limited, cramped, often made impossible owing to your physical condition. Here, when the mental desire is good, the field is unlimited. Any mental desire for truth, knowledge, be what it may, can be gratified in a most astonishing manner in this world. Be it good or bad, it will bring its results, and if the desire is bad it will grow in power and must be paid for; if good, it will grow in power also, and will bring strength and happiness with it.

I cannot emphasise to you too much that as you are, so you will be.

You are now, whilst on Earth, making your bodies for your next conditions. These are built up by your present lives by the quality of your thoughts. This world, which I have been in a long time now, is the closest thing imaginable to your Earth. It is full of mineral, vegetable, animal, and all forms of life. All the animals you have loved on Earth and educated to understanding, will be with you here. Those other animals who belong to no one in particular are here too, but they are in their own places. You will say, "Oh, then it is only a reflection of our world." It is not that way – the Earth is only a reflection of this world. Earth is not the lasting world. It is the training school. You are not only on Earth to amass riches and enjoy life, just for what it is; you are there to learn the truth about your own character, and how to control and develop it, to make full use of all Earth's beauties and pleasures, but you must be master, and not allow them to master you.

As I have said, looking back on my life here, I am satisfied with what has been done both in the personal and individual way and the bigger way. We spirit people have made great advances in our communication with Earth. We have been greatly and enormously helped by the physical strength of the spirits of all the young men and women who passed over during the recent fighting all over the world. Not only English, but all. They brought with them great physical power and determination, and we have been able, through this power, to break down many of the barriers which keep the two worlds apart.

These truths do not conform with the ideas of many people, but that is no reason for saying they are not true.

Truth is sometimes unexpected and none too pleasant, but it is always the most powerful, and will make itself known, no matter whether it brings pleasure or pain.

Go, each one of you, in reality or imagination, to the edge of a high cliff overlooking the sea. Let it be a bright, starry, frosty night, and go alone. Stand there and meditate. Look down upon the lights of any harbored, anchored boats, and think; then look up to the stars. You know where you are, and you are fully conscious of the flickering and movement of the lights on the boats.

You can see them. You are only a little way off … and perhaps you could make them hear if you called, but it would be easier to wait till the darkness breaks when they can see you without any effort on your part. That is how we spirit people are; conscious of those left behind, some willing to wait, others fighting and struggling to make themselves heard. It is only a little way from Earth, and between this, The Blue Island our spirit state and the Great Universe, there is as much distance as between you on the cliff and the farthest star.

We are only a little way on our journey – nothing yet forgotten – love still remaining.

14

The Great Ultimate

~

My life here has been a very normal, healthy and interesting affair, just as my life on Earth was. I have been invested with no powers generally attributed to spirits and fairies, I am still just an ordinary man with an ordinary plain, blunt outlook on life; the change has in no way altered me. The only change there is in me is my greater ability to move speedily and to act quickly. I am rejuvenated, and this is a condition which becomes more marked as time goes on.

Many people who give thought to these subjects, no matter what their particular point of view may be, ask the question, "To where is it all leading? What is to be our ultimate state?" This is a question of extreme difficulty to deal with on account of the limitations of the mind; both yours and ours.

I have explained to you that, as you are, so you will be when you come here. When here you will qualify for a further state, which will be your lot in due time, and there you will be exactly as you have made yourself by your life here. Better or worse, happier or more unhappy. From that you will go to a further state, another sphere if you like, and there again you will have made your own conditions.

In this further state you will be more self-contained; a word I use to express a state of being less dependent upon other people and things for development and progress. In this sphere you will again come in contact with your whole record. A record in full, of all former states: and from this sphere, if your record has qualified to the point of allowing it, you will be given the choice of returning to Earth again.

Reincarnating. If your record does not qualify for choice in this matter, you will be directed either to return or to continue according to what the Teachers, the Purified, consider will afford you most opportunity for recreating yourself and cleansing yourself in the necessary way. It is from this sphere that spirits return to Earth, but by the time the most progressed spirit has reached this state he has forgotten in detail his association with Earth. I cannot give the shortest period of time which would be necessary to reach this sphere, but the sojourn in the Real World after the Blue Island is a much longer period than that of mortal life; and in each sphere as progress is made the sojourn is longer.

The spirits who have reached this "return or stay sphere," and are purified and qualified in themselves. Those who stand the tests and pass out as Grade I, pass to another and altogether different and lighter land – and each becomes impersonal. Impersonal in the sense that they are no longer Jack Brown or Madge Black; they are now pure spirit people, and their former love, which had been a personal and individual thing, is no longer for one but equally for all. All are alike to all. The purest tissue of God's love binds one and all.

I have given a brief outline, sufficient for you to form your own ideas, your own mental pictures of Creation and its process. There would be no point in my going further into details, because if I were to give the facts you could not understand the conditions ruling in those advanced states. I am not able fully to understand them myself, for, as I have said, I am only a little way on my journey, but just far enough to grasp the intense beauty of life, and in life.

As one standing on a higher point than yourselves, and able to see a little more than you see, I can best explain to you that in these further states you receive not merely fifty, or sixty, or even a hundred per cent out of your lives in happiness and joy but you receive comparatively six hundred per cent. This is simply a graphic way of indicating the degree of happiness that obtains here.

Were I able to describe all the processes of our evolution many would say, "Oh, but I don't want that!"

But when progress has been made and intelligence brightened and reality is seen as reality, not as imagination, they will want it. If I said to an old man in an invalid chair that he could have a motor-bicycle, he'd say he preferred his invalid chair, but if he were to be a young, robust boy of nineteen again, which do you suppose he'd choose? This is the underlying principle.

Do you think that this scheme of the World is hateful and unkind and full of continual partings from all other spirits who are dear to each individually. I have said that there are "no" partings. It is always possible and customary for spirits to keep in close touch with each other on this side.

When the highest states of the impersonal are reached there are no partings from dear ones; only a wider opening of that same door of love – a higher, purer love, a Golden or God love – to admit not one or two or twenty but to embrace ALL.

15

CHRIST AND SPIRITUALISM

∼

U nfortunately the word "Spiritualism" has been associated with so many misconceptions that it affords scope for misinterpretation, and for this reason thousands of people misunderstand the word and suppose that it deals only with forms of fortune-telling and chicanery of all kinds, and must necessarily be wrong and dangerous, therefore the work of anti-Christ.

For this reason it is a barred subject. Not only do these people know nothing about it, but they are so horrified at the travesty they themselves have created that they would refuse to hear, see, or read a word upon the subject.

To all people who have knowledge of Spiritualism, this attitude is tiresome and regrettable, nevertheless it exists today, and in great force.

In my concluding chapter I want to say a few simple words on this point.

Spiritualism is not the work of anti-Christ.

All the teachings of Christ are to be found in the teachings of Spiritualism. Christ taught love amongst mankind, generous thought and generous help for one another. "Love thy neighbor as thyself," and so on. Spiritualism teaches these same doctrines. Christ was imbued with the Divine Spirit, and He laid down laws upon which His disciples were to model their lives and their work, and in those laws you will find the laws which govern Spiritualism.

Because one of the disciples was a dishonest, weak man, and because some of the workers since then, workers in the churches of various and many creeds have been, and are to this day, weak and sinful in their lives, you do not, any of you, think for one moment that the whole is bad and evil.

You realise that the teachings of Christ were of the highest.

Always He spoke of Love as the binding link and the force of all good. I want you to understand, perhaps for the first time, that Spiritualism is based upon the same foundations.

All its rules are rules given by Christ Himself. All the creeds existing upon Earth are based upon these same rules.

They vary in minor points considerably. What one will allow, another will condemn, and it is for the individual to decide which particular one of all is most fitting to himself. By his choice he will show his ability to grasp the meaning of God's laws, and according to his development so will he select.

The teachings of all alike are limited but some go farther, see farther, and understand more. Just as all roads may converge to a given point, so many creeds follow in the main the teachings of Christ. Some by narrow little roads and byways, some by wide roads, and some by main highways. Spiritualism is God's Main Highway.

The End

www.ingramcontent.com/pod-product-compliance
Lightning Source LLC
Chambersburg PA
CBHW031627040426
42452CB00007B/715